Antoni

GAUDÍ

© 1998 EDICIONES POLÍGRAFA, S. A.
Balmes, 54 - 08007 Barcelona

Text © Lluís Permanyer
© Melba Levick for all photographs,
except for the following:
Arxiu Nacional de Catalunya. Fons Brangulí, p. 4.
Arxiu Dr. Comas Llaberia, p. 5 below.
Museu Comarcal Salvador Vilaseca, Reus, p. 7.
Robert Justamante, pp. 12 and 13.
Pere Vivas, pp. 22, 23 above, 28, 29 and 54 above.
Juanjo Puente, p. 23 below.
Francesc Català-Roca, pp. 46 and 47.

English translation: Richard Rees

I.S.B.N.: 84-343-0857-6
Dep. legal: B. 1.940 - 1998 (Printed in Spain)

Printed by Filabo, S. A., Sant Joan Despí (Barcelona)

Antoni GAUDÍ

Text by **Lluís Permanyer**
Photographs by **Melba Levick**

EDICIONES POLÍGRAFA

*Gaudí at Barcelona Cathedral during the Corpus
Christi procession, June 11, 1924.*

INTRODUCTION

Gaudí was fortunate enough to be living at the right time, by virtue not only of the architectural style to which those of his generation contributed but also of the fact that he had at his disposal a site as attractive as Barcelona's Eixample (XIX-century urban extension). One example: the striking presence of La Pedrera could not possibly have ben achieved in the case of the Palau Güell.

Antoni Gaudí i Cornet was born on June 25, 1852. It is still not absolutely certain whether he came into this world in Reus or in Riudoms, a small village only four kilometres from the city; nonetheless, documentary evidence points to Reus. In terms of his origins, two factors were to have a decisive influence on his oeuvre. The first, the character of most natives to the region: "Gent de camp, gent de llamp" that is, a people typified by strength, determination, personality, obstinacy, tenacity: in a word, rauxa (impulse), that rauxa which in Catalonia constitutes an element which combines marvellously with seny (solid good sense), although what matters is the effect, in each individual case, of such arbitrary proportion. General Prim, to mention a figure of the period, is an illustrative example. And suffice it to recall the reaction of His Holiness Pope Pius IX when he was informed that only the Bishop of Pittsburgh had voted against the motion of raising papal infallibility to the category of dogma: "Naturally, he's from Reus" was the Pontiff's immortal comment. And he was right, for Doctor Domènec Veciana had been born in that city in 1816. Throughout the whole of his architectural career Gaudí acted as a true reusenc, since as a vanguardista he remained firmly faithful to and made absolutely no concessions regarding his aesthetic beliefs, despite incomprehension problems with clients, critics, the press, in short, with almost the entire society of his time. Despite such isolation, he staunchly stood his ground and his architecture was eventually accepted. On one occasion he openly admitted that he had managed to overcome all his defects except one, his irascibility. My belief is that not only did he not attempt to overcome it; he positively cultivated it.

The second factor was a family one: according to Gaudí, the fact that his father was a coppersmith endowed him with a natural sense of architectural space, which permitted him to think directly in three dimensions rather than in the two to which he was restricted when drawing up plans.

An event of capital importance took place in 1869: in order to complete his secondary education he was sent to a school in Barcelona. And from that moment onwards Gaudí would never move from a city that would provide him with everything he needed.

Both at secondary school and at the Escola d'Arquitectura, which had only recently been created, Gaudí revealed that imbalance so typical of certain types of genius. He was neither a brilliant nor a docile pupil; nor did he recognise any of his teachers as masters. He worked as a draughtsman with Francisco de Paula del Villar whom, through the irony of fate, he had to replace when the latter resigned as architect of the Sagrada Família. As soon as he left architecture school he collaborated with Josep Fontserè, a professional he esteemed and respected and in whose studio he contributed to the realisation of certain details of the major project in which Fontserè was involved, the Ciutadella Park. But the person who was destined to influence Gaudí's basic training was the architect Joan Martorell, with whom he worked on a number of major projects. He also came into contact with consummate craftsmen such as Eudald Puntí, with whom he designed a display cabinet for a collection of gloves by Esteve Comellas. Eusebi Güell was deeply moved by the piece, which led eventually to the encounter between the genius and his future maecenas. So astonished was Güell by the originality and beauty of that cabinet that he did not rest until he had met its author in person. The meeting between Gaudí and Güell was destined to be providential, not so much for the prosaic, even mercenary reason that the latter provided the architect with a good number of far from insignificant briefs but rather because of the complete trust Güell placed in Gaudí and the total freedom in which he allowed him to work. Furthermore, the aristocrat needed someone who would allow him to distinguish himself socially, precisely at a time when the most accepted way to do so was by building huge constructions. And there was nobody like Gaudí when it came to ensuring that the future Count of Güell could not possibly be confused with a run-of-the-mill bourgeois. Neither criticism, insulting jibes nor scorn affected Gaudí. The architect was so sure of himself that he felt only disdain for those unable to appreciate his work. Being an avantguardista meant going ahead of the rest of his generation, a fact that explains

Eusebi Güell i Bacigalupi, Gaudí's great friend and maecenas, 1915.

Early in the century Doctor César Comas captured this astonishing image of the entirely rural surroundings of the Sagrada Família.

LA CASA-PEDRERA

— Està bé, tot m'agrada, però no us puc llogar el pis!
— Per què?
— Perquè amb aquestes baranes tan artístiques no em seria possible mai posar domassos als balcons.

The famous cartoonist Junceda, who was harshly critical of Modernisme, *also satirised La Pedrera in the review* En Patufet.

A cartoonist employed by the satirical magazine L'Esquella de la Torratxa *made this malicious prediction in 1912: the building would eventually become a kind of multi-storey zeppelin park.*

The outstanding painter and cartoonist Martí Bas, in L'Esquella *in 1937, suggested that the anarchists had not burnt down the Sagrada Família because it was still unfinished.*

his own solitude and the incomprehension and animosity his work provoked.

Gaudí was so self-assured that he ignored not only criticism but even building regulations: the municipal architect, Rovira i Trias, refused to approve the Palau Güell; Casa Calvet was higher than regulations allowed; work on Casa Batlló was halted since it had been begun without authorisation; the dimensions of La Pedrera went far beyond permitted limits and, as if this were not enough, a column at street level blocked the passage of passers-by. Far from allowing himself to be dissuaded, however, the architect confronted the authorities. In all honesty, however, it must be said that the officials of the time rose to the occasion and in all cases tolerated his excesses without adopting coercive measures. The solution adopted with regard to Casa Milà (La Pedrera) would still be exemplary even today, since the authorities recognised that it was an exceptional work which could not be fettered by the regulations in force.

The people of Barcelona were astonished, even stupefied, although they had become more or less accustomed to such excesses; other architects had also designed striking, even controversial, façades. People not native to the city, however, were not so well prepared. I think it is revealing that the owner of a modernista house from Granada should have put up the following, very expressive sign: "The present owner is not responsible for this façade". Unamuno fired his broadsides against the urban landscape of Barcelona with insults far stronger even than fachadosa (façade-infested). Despite the fact that he was in New York, Juan Ramón Jiménez did not hesitate to describe modernista Barcelona as "the victim of a Catalan architect's nightmare". Valle Inclán, indignant at the sight of the Palau Güell, described it thus in one of his novels: "funereal, barbarous and Catalan". When Clemenceau, the politician and French Prime Minister, discovered Passeig de Gràcia he was so horrified that he left immediately for Paris. On his arrival at the French capital, the first thing he did was summon a press conference, and told the gathered journalists that Barcelona was an awful city where they were building houses for dinosaurs and dragons.

I wonder why the buildings Gaudí constructed in the north of Spain never became as important as his Barcelona works. I suspect that this was due not so much to the influence of the client as to the fact that the architect monitored none of them on site, which in his case would have repercussions on the results, since he would react to knowledge of the site and the way the building work developed. It is well known that he would sometimes change his mind in mid execution of a project and improvise on the spot. Evidence of this is his intervention on Mallorca Cathedral, in which the force of his participation, almost a manifesto, can be clearly appreciated.

We do not know why Gaudí never married. It may not be far-fetched, however, to suggest that while not a born misogynist, he became one. Because of a broken love affair? Who knows? The fact is that he devoted himself entirely to architecture and lived only for his work. To the extent that in 1910 it is likely that too many briefs and responsibilities caused a deep depression that led to anaemia, which left him defenceless against Maltese fever. So serious was his condition that he was on the point of death and even dictated his last will and testament. I suspect that all this led him to the realisation, upon reflection, that by then he had produced sufficient works to be able to refuse any further briefs and concentrate on the Sagrada Família. Evidence of this is the fact that on the death of his father and his niece, with whom he shared his home, he decided to move to his studio on the site of the cathedral he was so enthusiastically building. Death came upon him suddenly: one mid afternoon he was walking, as was his custom, to the Church of Sant Felip Neri to pray when he was run over by a tram. No one recognised him, he was dressed almost like a tramp and no taxi driver was prepared to take him to hospital. Furthermore, once there he was not administered the emergency treatment he needed. It would have done no good in any case, since his injuries were of necessity fatal.

Gaudí still had to suffer his purgatory, however; a purgatory imposed by the militants of Noucentisme. The following generation detested Modernisme and Gaudí alike. In fact, the first to champion him were Dalí, who described his architecture as "edible", and the Surrealists.

His true recognition on a worldwide scale did not come until 1952, when the American specialist Collins presented a major exhibition of Gaudí's work in New York. A fundamental contribution in this sense was also the unbounded passion and fascination for Gaudí on the part of the Japanese, who admire above all the way he recreated nature.

It is important to know that the origin of this inspiration is to be found in the rheumatic fever from which the architect suffered as a child; he was unable to join in the other children's games and, forced to remain immobile, he had no alternative but to exercise his sense of observation, which allowed him to discover the spectacle of creation all around him. Hence his love of the curve, since he proclaimed that there are no straight lines in nature. He was capable not only of falling in love with a flower but also of taking it as the ornamental motif with which to decorate an entire façade. And when it came to choosing a landscape, he swore that the Mediterranean had no rival since its light, the fundamental element in sculpture and above all architecture, is unequalled.

Gaudí is today known and admired all over the world, and as a man he was unique, even somewhat eccentric, although not to draw attention to himself. This was simply an aspect of his nature. A genius.

BIOGRAPHICAL SUMMARY

1852 Antoni Gaudí i Cornet, son of the cooper of Riudoms, is born in Reus on June 25.

1869 Moves to Barcelona to pursue his secondary education.

1873 Begins his architectural studies and collaborates with the master builder Fontserè.

1876 His mother dies. Gaudí works as draughtsman for the architect Francisco de Paula del Villar.

1878 Graduates as an architect. Strikes up a friendship with Eusebi Güell.

1881 Designs the La Obrera Mataronesa factory.

1885 A cholera epidemic in Barcelona forces him to live for a number of months in Sant Feliu de Codines, in the Vallès Oriental, which affords him the opportunity to become familiar with the spectacular Sant Sadurní mountain, near Gallifa, probably the source of inspiration for "La Pedrera".

1888 Designs the Compañía Transatlántica Pavilion for the Barcelona World Fair.

1891 Travels to León and Astorga for the Casa de los Botines and Palacio Episcopal projects. Travels also to Málaga and Tangiers with the Marquis of Comillas with the idea of building the African Catholic Missions.

1900 Casa Calvet wins the annual Barcelona City Hall Award. He decorates one of the salons in the Café Torino, on the corner of Passeig de Gràcia and Granvia. Designs the I Misteri de Glòria for the Monumental Rosary of Montserrat.

1903 Travels to Mallorca to restore the Cathedral.

1904 Xalet Catllaràs, in Pobla de Lillet.

1905 Moves to the Park Güell with his father and niece.

1906 His father dies.

1907 Designs the monument to Jaume I, in Barcelona's Gothic Quarter.

1910 Designs to monument to Jaume Balmes, in Vic. Only two street lamps are built, conceived in collaboration with the architect Josep M. Jujol. His delicate health forces him to rest in Vic. Exhibition of his works in Paris, sponsored by Eusebi Güell.

1911 Contracts Maltese fever. Period of repose in Puigcerdà. Close to death, he dictates his will.

1912 His niece dies. Thrones for the Church of Santa Maria de Blanes, which were destroyed during the Civil War.

1918 Sketch for the monument to Enric Prat de la Riba in Castellterçol, where he was born and is now buried.

1925 Goes to live in his workshop at the Sagrada Família.

1926 Run over by a tram on June 7. Dies three days later in the Hospital de la Santa Creu. Buried on June 12 in the Sagrada Família crypt.

1936 With the outbreak of the Civil War, not only was the Sagrada Família crypt burnt and the tombs of Bocabella and Gaudí violated, even the offices and documents of the Gaudí archive were destroyed.

Antoni Gaudí, 1878.

CASA VICENS

Overall view of the façade, from Carrer de les Carolines, revealing its striking personality.

In 1878 work began on the project for a single-family house on which the architect did not engrave his signature, thus stating that he considered it unfinished, until 1883. Construction work, supervised by Gaudí himself, continued until 1888. The brief came from Manuel Vicens Montaner for a house to be built on a site at no. 24, Carrer de les Carolines, in the Gràcia district. The owner was a tile manufacturer, a metier to which Gaudí pays homage by audaciously and imaginatively employing these materials to give personality to an ornamental ensemble under the sign of "horror vacui". The work consisted basically of a house with three façades and a sizeable garden.

As the years passed, urban planning needs, such as the widening of the street, and others led to mutilations and transformations, although luckily none of these was substantial in nature. Some took place during Gaudí's own lifetime and it was the architect himself who supervised the inevitable changes. Thus the wall and the railings which enclosed the site were removed (fragments of the railings are preserved in the Park Güell, in the Museu Güell and in the school of the same name). In 1946 part of the garden was sold as the plot for a block of flats and in 1962 the small temple dedicated to Santa Rita was also sold and another block built in its place. While the architecture specialist Joan Bassegoda detects traces of a freely interpreted far-eastern influence, such as the Chinese-style blinds, the architect and historian Ignasi de Solà-Morales speaks of influences of the Mediterranean and Arab traditions in the compositional methods.

The impact of Casa Vicens on the unsuspecting passer-by is certainly great, two factors constituting the forceful personality of the house: forms and colour. The forms stand out especially on the upper floors and crowning elements. A series of vertical alignments, which reinforce both the filled and empty sections, converge towards an asymmetrical ensemble of sloping planes and domes. But while these structures are certainly powerful, no less potent is another fundamental element: polychromy. Gaudí basically employed iron, stone, brick and tiles with true mastery. Polychromy appears as essential as the basis for ornamentation, while also highlighting and emphasising certain aspects of the structure. Needless to say, the complex as a whole fascinates us, by virtue not only of the enormous personality of the concept on which the project is based but also of its dazzling display of far from arbitrary colours, which are subtly applied only to strategic points. Equally remarkable is the creative, enriching

The use of the facing endows
the façade with its original
personality.

Dining room. None of this would have been possible without the collaboration of consummate craftsmen.

Ceiling of the gallery adjacent to the dining room.
Each design element pays clear homage to functionality.

dialogue into which the different materials enter, thanks to the harmony which the architect managed to impose.

While the exterior impresses the observer with its unmistakable personality, the interior is the product of an ornamental concept which operates on the basis of addition and leaves no corner untouched, resulting in a total work,

a style that Gaudí had just begun to apply which would develop into a characteristic of his oeuvre. The interior spaces constitute a world in themselves, each one typified by its own differentiated ambience. Thus specialists agree on the clear Nazarene influence on the smokers' room. Profuse decoration and prefect finishes are the most outstanding

aspects. Experienced craftsmen gave of their best, as did artists such as the painter Josep Torrescassana and the sculptor Antoni Riba, all working in harmony under the demanding surveillance of Gaudí.

Casa Vicens was awarded the prestigious annual Barcelona City Hall Prize.

EL CAPRICHO. COMILLAS

General view of the house and tower.

In 1883 Máximo Díaz de Quijano, a bachelor who had made his fortune in the Americas, commissioned Gaudí to design a summer residence. The choice may be explained by family and neighbour ties. Indeed, Díaz de Quijano was the brother-in-law of Claudio López y López, first Marquis of Comillas, and on a neighbouring plot the Catalan architect Joan Martorell had built the Sobrellano Palace for Antonio López y Piélago.

The controversy continues to this day as to whether or not Gaudí visited the elegant town of Santander. Joan Bassegoda, the recognised authority on Gaudí's work, has provided evidence of at least one visit there, in the company of the great Barcelona sculptor Llimona. In any case, one thing is a visit and quite another is on-site monitoring of the construction work. Indeed, from the very outset Gaudí had proposed that the works be directed by his colleague Cristòfor Cascante Colom. This choice was not a gratuitous one, since Cascante was a professional Gaudí had met while at university and with whom he had enjoyed a good working relationship at Fontserè's studio, where they had collaborated on minor development projects for the Ciutadella Park. Furthermore, there was something else in his favour: Cristòfor Cascante had been living for some time in Santander, where he had carried out a number of projects. Gaudí could therefore breathe easily, despite the distance and difficult communications.

El Capricho was completed in 1885, the product of an uneventful building process. The only incident, in fact, was the sudden death of the owner, who was thus robbed of the chance ever to enjoy his original summer residence. The house was subsequently inherited by his relatives. In 1914 some rather unscrupulous alterations were made. Much later restoration work became necessary, which was begun around 1970 but never completed. The Consejería de Cultura of the Cantabrian Government acquired the building in 1984 as a cultural centre, which implied the will to restore it. This, however, never went beyond good intentions. In

1988 it was converted into a restaurant, a fact which ensured its preservation.

The site on which the fortunate bachelor wanted Gaudí to build his house was by no means easy to negotiate, due among other things to its steep slope. El Capricho is based on a long ground plan measuring 15×36 metres and consists of three levels: the semi-basement, accommodating the kitchen and the servants' quarters; the main floor, with the dining room, salons and bedrooms; and the attic. Due to the slope, the architect was obliged to supply the house with a visually very solid base, rather like a pedestal, built of ashlars laid in wide horizontal strips. This socle marks a strong distinction between the building and surrounding nature. The façade open to the four winds, characterised by youthful eclecticism, is based on naked brick with a striking, repeated decorative element: Valencia tiles with a sunflower motif. Other outstanding elements are the wrought-iron work on freely styled eyecatching balconies, classical guillotine-type windows that emit musical sounds when opened, and above all the tower, which endows a complex that would otherwise have remained half-hidden with force and elegance.

Detail of the crowning elements with chimneys and ventilations shafts, and the classical guillotine-shaped windows.

THE GÜELL ESTATE PAVILIONS

*General view from
Avinguda de Pedralbes.*

The Güell estate pavilions stand at no. 7, Avinguda de Pedralbes. The origins of the huge property owned by Gaudí's maecenas go back a generation earlier, for it was Joan Güell i Ferrer (1800-1876) an industrialist and businessman, who purchased two extensive estates in the Les Corts district: Can Feliu and Torre Baldiró. His son and heir, Eusebi Güell i Bacigalupi (1846-1918), was able to considerably extend the property by acquiring the adjoining estate known as Can Cuyàs de la Riera. This was in 1883, and the following year Güell requested Gaudí's intervention. The architect built a series of highly functional constructions, such as a wall to mark the limits of the property, three

entrance gates, an arbour and a fountain, as well as altering and refurbishing the rural mansion.

Two of the gates ceased to have any purpose after the estate had been divided; one of them now stands beside the Biology Faculty while the other, which was demolished and later exactly reconstructed in 1953, may be admired at the Chemistry Faculty. The main gate was the most important and the one which reveals that for Gaudí no project could be considered prosaic, since he became involved body and soul in all his briefs. Hence this gate has been judged the most spectacular example of *modernista* design. The railings are dominated by an imposing dragon in beaten iron which receives visitors with its jaws wide open, the jealous keeper of the enchanted garden of the Hesperides. And it is in terms of this same symbology that the pinnacle crowned by an antimony orange tree must be interpreted, featuring the owner's initial, "G", framed by wild roses. To the left stands the pavilion-shaped caretaker's lodge and, to the right, the original stables and ring which now house the Càtedra Gaudí (Gaudí Chair). The simplicity of the structure and the restrained decoration, which despite its economy is no less effective, are examples of Gaudí's gift for creating highly personal spaces, in this case through the use of parabolic vaults and arches.

On the threshold of the nineteen-twenties, part of the estate was set aside as the site for the Palau Reial (Royal Palace). Hence in 1983 a fountain by Gaudí, which had been given up for lost, was found intact beneath a thick blanket of vegetation in what had formerly been the royal gardens.

*Crowning element of
ventilation shaft and
exterior walls with
detail of gypsum-moulded
false mosaic.*

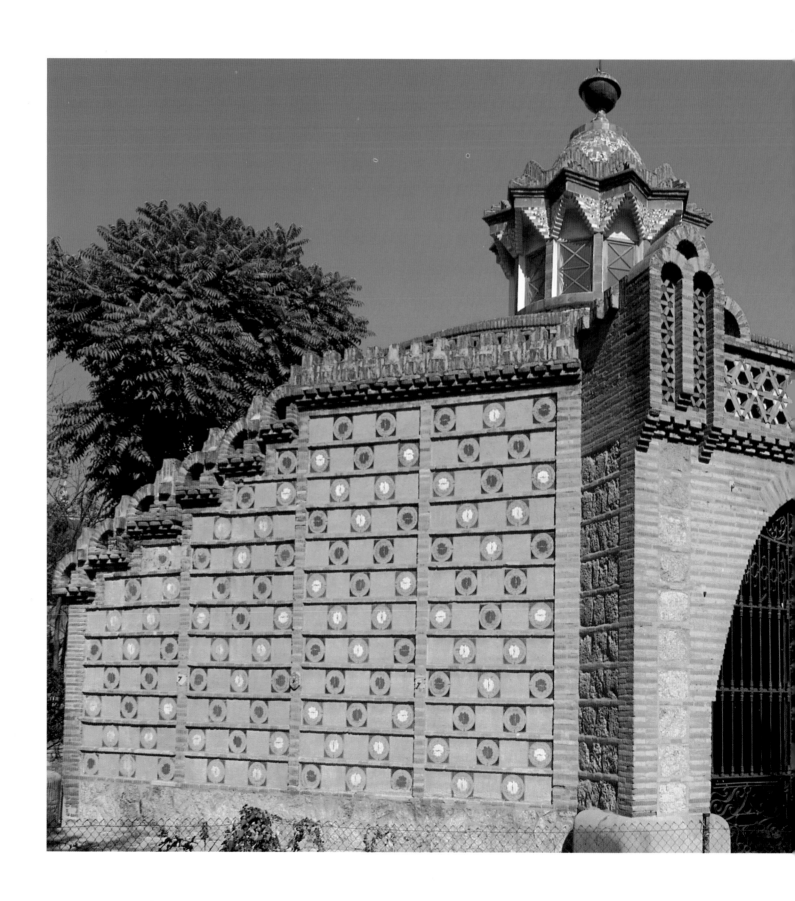

The Güell Estate Pavilions. The stables nave, which today houses the Càtedra Gaudí.

Detail of the dome.

PALAU GÜELL

Fragment of the main façade.

So impressed was Güell with Gaudí's work that he immediately commissioned a major work from the architect, nothing less than his own residence: a palace.

Gaudí began work in 1886 and the construction was completed in 1889. For the project, he enlisted the collaboration of numerous craftsmen of renown.

The main façade is of exceptional quality, although there is no deliberate innovative will in evidence here, unlike in the cases of Casa Batlló or "La Pedrera". It is based on slight asymmetry dominated by discreet horizontality, also imposed on the crowning elements. The most striking features are the ornaments: wrought iron here fulfils a mission of great importance since it is the counterpoint that tempers the rather stark effect of the openings and figures as the protagonist of the spectacular coat-of-arms of Catalonia that presides over the ground floor, framed by the two doors.

The main entrance leads also to the basement, which Gaudí designed as the coach house. Nobody could have imagined that such a secondary part of the building could be so beautiful.

The first floor accommodates a series of salons around the main feature of the palace: the great staircase covered by a parabolic arch featuring an unexpected celestial dome that links the floors together and to the exterior, evoking by virtue of its configuration the distant firmament. A structural element that immediately catches the visitor's eye are the one hundred and twenty-seven columns of extraordinary texture. It would be impossible to describe in detail all the ornamental details that cover this space. Suffice it to say that it is here that the visitor must have all his wits about him in order not to miss anything.

The rear façade is highly creative and original, outstanding elements of which being the materials used and the innovative gallery. Wood, iron and glazed ceramics are very well combined here,

Details of the arches and the
wrought-iron work that adorns them.

in terms both of qualities and colours. The most striking feature is the simple parasol obtained through the juxtaposition of wooden slats.

The greatest surprise kept in store for us, however, is the magic roof, an often secondary space which Gaudí chose precisely to reveal the extent to which the imagination is capable, with just a few elements and at a very low cost, of attaining an exceptionally expressive plastic effect. What is an essentially utilitarian complex — chimneys and ventilators — the architect transformed into a sculptural paradise; moreover, a sculptural paradise that heralded "La Pedrera" and even the coming century of avant-garde art. Each of the pieces imposes its presence by virtue of their striking, expressive forms, of the innovative use of a series of materials and of the plastic impact of the polychrome facing. Many of these elements were not completed by Gaudí, and in 1994 the architect Antonio González Moreno-Navarro, head of the Heritage Preservation Department of the Barcelona County Council, owner of the palace,

invited several artists and architects to re-cover the pieces with broken fragments of ceramic, the technique known as *trencadís de ceràmica*. The result was largely satisfactory.

In 1906 Eusebi Güell abandoned the palace as his residence. Shortly after the end of the Civil War, Barcelona was on the verge of losing this architectural

gem, since an American millionaire was negotiating its removal stone-by-stone to his country. Luckily, the County Council acquired it in 1954 and converted the building into the city's Theatre Museum. Not only have they respected the palace in an exemplary way but they have also not hesitated in spending vast sums of money on its impeccable restoration.

The rear façade is more
avant-garde in style.

Filtered light enriches
the interior.

The parabolic dome
is one of the most
spectacular surprises.

THE ASTORGA EPISCOPAL PALACE

*The main façade, clearly
reminiscent of Neogothic castles.*

This is a minor work whose main point of interest is the complex and eventful construction process.

Joan Grau, immediately after having been appointed Bishop of the diocese of Astorga, saw his palace destroyed by fire. For this reason, and also because he was a native of Rues and was even acquainted with Gaudí, in 1886 he commissioned the architect to draw up the project for his new residence. Gaudí was delighted to accept, although he warned Grau that the Palau Güell was occupying so much of his time that he would be unable to supervise the work in Astorga. In 1887 he sent the plans to the prelate, who was very impressed by them.

For bureaucratic reasons, the project had to be approved by the San Fernando Fine Arts Academy, Madrid. The Academy stipulated that the roof structure had to be altered as a fire prevention measure and that a number of minor modifications had to be made. Gaudí complied. At the second revision, however, the Academy stated that the modifications were not sufficient, a fact which triggered Gaudí's legendary temper.

Between 1889 and 1893 Gaudí visited the works several times. The latter year, however, the bishop died and the construction process was halted. Shortly afterwards bitter disagreements arose between the architect and the episcopal authorities that, given his irascible character, led to his irrevocable resignation. The architect recounted his own version of events to the Infanta Isabella of Bourbon while showing her around the Sagrada Família: "Madam, I did not resign; I was dismissed."

And it was then that the difficult process of completing the building really began. In 1894 the architect Francisco Blanch was commissioned to continue with the project, but the works were immediately halted. They were not resumed until 1899, this time with the architect Manuel Hernández in charge, who continued until 1904, although he never visited Astorga. In 1905, the new bishop begged Gaudí to return; but the master excused himself by saying that he was overloaded with work. The prelate turned to the Marquis of Comillas for help, but Gaudí held firm to his decision not to accept. Shortly afterwards, the work was entrusted to the architect Ricardo García Guerreta, who unfortunately crowned the building with a roof very different from the one Gaudí had designed.

Once the project had been completed, the curios thing is that the building was never used as an episcopal palace. During the Civil War it was an artillery barracks and suffered some damage. In the sixties it was converted into the Road to Santiago Museum.

The most impressive aspect of the project is the way in which Gaudí solved the difficult problem of creating a large, detached and highly visible building that would set up a positive relationship with the neighbouring cathedral. It is very much like a Neogothic castle in appearance, an effect enhanced by the unusual moat, the buttresses and the towers. The use of rough, white Bierzo granite creates a pleasing aesthetic effect, while connoisseurs of Gaudí's work will be surprised by the symmetry of the façade, bordering on monotony. The palace is based on a ground plan in the form of a Greek cross, with a large central space that serves effectively as a hall. Once inside, the visitor is impressed by the tasteful use of dark-coloured glazed brick.

View of the palace interior. In the sixties the building was converted into the Road to Santiago Museum.

THE TERESIANES SCHOOL

Wrought-iron entrance gate.

It was in 1888 that Gaudí was made an unusual proposition. He received a visit from Father Enric d'Ossó i Cervelló, who hailed from Vinebre and who entrusted him with the task of continuing with a project which had begun badly: the author of the original plans — we know neither his name nor whether he was an architect or master builder — had thrown in the towel having erected no more than the first floor of the building. I suspect that Gaudí was intrigued by his prospective client, founder of the Company of Santa Teresa, devoted to education; I further suspect that his being a man of the Church also had a favourable effect on the architect, plus the fact that, like himself, d'Ossó was from Tarragona. He would also have been attracted to the idea of building a religious school. Furthermore, I would contend that Gaudí liked the somewhat complex challenge of continuing with a project already in the process of construction, limited by a very restricted budget and an extremely tight deadline set for the inauguration of the centre. Suppositions apart, the fact is that he unhesitatingly rose to the challenge and set to work at once.

The site had been acquired by d'Ossó in what was then the township of Sant Gervasi de Cassoles, today Carrer de Ganduxer in the Barcelona district of Sant Gervasi. What I find most attractive about the building that Gaudí constructed is the ductile way in which he made it adapt to the needs, which on the other hand were very prosaic, of such a particular client. This is further evidence of the architect's amazing versatility, which allowed him to give free rein to his vividly heterodox imagination, surrendering to the temptation of embarking on an ornate decorative adventure while keeping to the budget and respecting the function of the school. The result is a magnificent and charactersitically Gaudinian building. Needless to say, relations between two such obstinate individuals as Gaudí and d'Ossó were fragile in the extreme; an example of this is the merited rebuff the founder received when he complained of the cost of some of the materials: Gaudí told him to go to... the devil, since the building process was the architect's responsibility. Despite everything, however, and despite the scant resources, the school for girls was opened in 1890.

The Teresianes School is characterised by sobriety of form and the austerity of its interior. Indeed, on a prismatic structure, regular in ground plan, Gaudí restricted himself to building smooth

*Overall view. The criteria of
austerity imposed by the owner
were no obstacle to the creation
of an imposing façade.*

The succession of diaphragmatic parabolic arches.

walls of brick and rubblework, attaining maximum expressivity through the restrained resource of repeating the same module along the sixty metres of façade. And yet, despite such a minimalist concept, the overall effect, in which there is a combination of both parabolic and non-parabolic windows, shutters flush with the surface creating the sensation of a curtain wall, crenellations and pinnacles, is attractive and imposing, subtly balanced by the counterpoint of a light chiaroscuro. Inside, Gaudí took this ability to create an unmistakable style a step further with the mise-en-scène of a minimum of possible elements. And it is thus, through a moving display of essentialness, that the architect composed a series of spaces, to the enriching charm and magic of which no visitor can possibly be indifferent. There is the magnificent combination of an interior patio which distributes natural light everywhere — functional areas and linear corridors alike —, although I must confess that I am fascinated, above all, by the seductive effect created by these corridors marked by the narrowness of their highly personal parabolic arches, which call the visitor in while offering a world of sensations and emotions with which even the least sensitive might identify.

CASA DE LOS BOTINES, LEON

General view of the building.

While Gaudí was working on the Astorga project, he was accosted by two businessmen, Simón Fernández and Mariano Andrés, who commissioned him to design a large building for the centre of León to house their business as well as including their own homes and a number of flats to let. The site, in a prominent position within the city's urban tissue, looked onto the Plaza de San Marcelo.

Once Gaudí had accepted, the project was completed in an unusually short space of time. Although Gaudí paid the occasional visit to the site, in order to avoid travelling and to forestall misunderstandings he entrusted the building work to Claudi Alsina, with whom he furnished a series of highly detailed plans. All the materials suppliers, as well as the workforce, were Catalans, a fact that caused certain unrest in the city.

The Casa de los Botines is a striking edifice by virtue of the fact not only that it looks onto a square but also that it is exposed to the four winds. The basements are surrounded by a wide moat, like the one in Astorga, in order to take maximum advantage of the natural light. The ground floor was given over to the offices and commercial dependencies of the Fernández and Andrés textile business whose founder, Joan Homs Botinàs, had been a banker. His second surname, slightly distorted, provided the official name for the building. The first floor contained the private residences of both proprietors. The next two floors above accommodated four rented flats each while the top floor was simply an attic. The slate of the gable roof offsets the grey rough stone of the façade. At each of the four corners of the solid-looking square building stands a cylindrical vertical tower, much lighter in appearance than the rest of the edifice.

The main entrance is embellished with a large sculpture depicting St. George and the Dragon, a motif much beloved of Gaudí. The piece was modelled in gypsum by Llorenç Matamala from Barcelona and sculpted on site in León by Cantó.

Gaudí designed the interiors of the ground-floor offices, although subsequent uses of the space have mutilated the original layout.

The plans are still preserved today thanks to a coincidence: while some alterations were being made, part of the

St. George fighting the Dragon. Modelled in gypsum by Llorenç Matamala of Barcelona and sculpted in León by Cantó, it adorns the main entrance.

sculptures fell off and in 1951 it was decided to restore them. During the process, a lead tube was found deposited in the façade containing the plans and, true to the ritual, newspapers and coins of the period.

This work has been related stylistically to the Astorga episcopal palace by virtue not only of its clear Neogothic influence but also of the materials used and the austerity of the façade.

The building has been the property of the Caja de Ahorros y Monte de Piedad de León savings bank since 1929.

CASA CALVET

Symmetry, the undulating top and the gallery predominate on the main façade.

In 1898 the widow of the textile industrialist Pere Màrtir Calvet i Carbonell entrusted Gaudí with the task of designing a family house on the site at no. 48, Carrer de Casp. Although the plot was an undistinguished one between party walls, it was located in the heart of the *Dreta de l'Eixample* district, where the city's haute bourgeoisie of the time lived. I have no idea why Gaudí decided to make this his most conventional and least audacious work (indeed, an uninitiated passer-by would probably not even imagine that this façade is by Gaudí although, of course, he would recognise it as a work of *Modernisme*). In view of the architect's uncompromising personality, it is inconceivable that he would have succumbed to pressure from the Calvets' demand for an unobtrusive though extraordinarily high-quality façade, as certain malicious tongues would have us believe.

The façade, consisting entirely of partially roughhewn ashlars, is surprising in that this was the only occasion on which Gaudí cultivated symmetry, since he disapproved of what he considered an exercise in repetition. The rhythm established between full and empty spaces, between smooth stone and ornamentation, strikes the observer as very balanced and functional. The gallery on the lower part of the façade is its most outstanding element, a daring piece clearly intended to be noticed by virtue of its fruitful combination of wrought iron and stone which trace out historiated decorative elements, treated realistically and allowing us to recognise a cypress, an olive tree, the coat of arms of Catalonia and horns of plenty. One must look upwards to the top of the building, however, to discover its other most spectacular feature, in the form of a double pinion which breaks the predominantly linear arrangement. It is precisely here that the architect placed the building's most original balconies, with their corresponding gins to hoist furniture, which anticipate the style

The lift is the most outstanding element in the entrance hall.

of Casa Batlló balconies on Passeig de Gràcia. Crowning the façade are a number of decorative elements closely linked to the personality of Andreu Calvet, since they feature the heads of *Sant Pere Màrtir*, a reference to the owner's father, *Sant Genís Notari* and *Sant Genís Còmic*, the two patron saints of Vilassar, Calvet's home town. Further personal allusions include the columns framing the main entrance, sculpted in the form of bobbins which evoke the family business, and the mushrooms above the gallery balustrade which pay tribute to the *pater familias*' favourite hobby.

The vestibule is an impressive complex, beginning with the large cross-

A detail of the decoration of the lift shaft.

*The entrance hall
is a first-class
ornamental complex.*

*A detail of the staircase.
Wrought-iron, decorated
ceramic, joinery and
ornamental sculpture
combine with and
enhance each other.*

shaped wrought-iron door knockers which when used strike a bedbug, in those days considered the embodiment of Evil: invariably associated with filth, its bite spread disease. The parapet tiling, the well-turned spiral columns, the paintings on the ceiling, the bench, the mirror, but above all the lift, an astonishing sculpture in wood enriched with wrought iron, all figure among the major attractions of Casa Calvet and are magnificent and humbling examples of Gaudí's prowess as a designer, which we appreciate both in small details such as the spyholes and door handles and in the avant-garde furniture which heralds that of the Palau Güell. For his client's house the architect created formidable pieces of organic, sensually curvilinear furniture in oak wood, manufactured by the highly credited Casas & Bardés firm of joiners, some of which can now be admired in Gaudí's Museum-House. It is only relatively recently, however, that we have been blessed with the good fortune to be able to savour a space which had hitherto been strictly private: the owner's offices which occupied the whole of the building's ground floor. This exquisite space, meticulously designed by Gaudí, has been preserved intact and recently transformed into the Restaurant Casa Calvet, whose proprietors have respected and potentiated such a striking ambience with a cuisine thoroughly in keeping with its setting. Outstanding in the dining area, for example, are the benches in the lobby, the double benches against the wall, the joinery separating the different areas of the former office, the counter, the door handles, the beams, etc. Joan Bassegoda tells us that the furniture is dovetailed,

that is, fitted together without the use of a single nail. We may also observe fascinating details from another period, such as the list of payments which figures on the outer frame of one of the private room doors. Although it is a shame that a certain amount of imitation has taken place, such as in the toilets, which can only lead to confusion, it is nonetheless thrilling to be able to experience a fully operational work by Gaudí and discover the absolute modernity of certain prosaic details, such as the great naked beam and the ivory-like tone of the brick walls which contrasts with the pink touch of the border.

THE COLONIA GÜELL CRYPT

*Overall view and detail
of the church Gaudí
built for the Güell
industrial complex.*

The carved, slanting
columns constitute a
language of their own.

Detail of one of the stained-glass windows.

Eusebi Güell had resolved to create a large-scale textile complex on a property covering some thirty hectares. Its pioneering character converted it into the first industrial-residential estate to be built in Spain. Not only did it contain the factory and the homes, of course, but also sports fields, choir associations, cooperatives, theatre, and so on. And since the church soon became too small for a population that was growing so quickly, Güell decided to entrust his much admired Gaudí with the construction of the new temple. The foundation stone was not laid until 1908 and the church not consecrated until 1915, although it was still unfinished. In order to understand such a delay, it is necessary to know that the architect was concerned with creating a truly brilliant, revolutionary work, that posed him a whole series of problems; nevertheless, the result was a masterpiece.

The innovations are several: perhaps the most complex is the fact that a general, oblong ground plan was adopted, based on the hierarchical order of structures. This freestanding building which consists of a ground floor only which, although not subterranean, is endowed with a cavernous air. On the other hand, the astonishing porticoed atrium bears a very close relationship to the nearby pine wood. The intimate quality of the building thus acquires an unprecedentedly prominent position: serpentine arcs, hyperbolic paraboloid vaults, both traditional and heterodox, sinuous ribs, leaning columns, etc. Into this context the architect introduced the four basalt columns formed from the pure, simple juxtaposition of three stones, representing respectively the base, the shaft and the capital, a hitherto unparalleled innovation. And despite the fact that the pervading atmosphere is that of a cave and the light does not uniformly bathe the whole of the interior, it is filtered through a set of highly suggestive stained-glass windows; this light, measured and of extraordinary quality, is the touch that endows the interior with its magic quality.

And in accordance with the determination to refuse to consider any kind of material ignoble, we note how Gaudí used elements recovered from rubbish tips, for instance, the window grilles, which are an ingenious assembly of old knitting needles. This is a concept characteristic of Jujol, who designed the central altar, of which only the shrine remains, and the side altar on the left. The altar on the right is the work of the architect Isidre Puig Boada. A further outstanding element here are the pews, a subtle combination of iron and wood.

PARK GÜELL

The staircase endows the itinerary with an initiatory air.

Park Güell is one of Gaudí's master-pieces, despite the fact that not only was the project never completed but it was doomed to failure from the very outset. Even so, Gaudí's contribution to the project was finished, displaying all the meaning and force characteristic of his work. In 1962 Park Güell was catalogued as an artistic monument by the Barcelona City Hall; in 1969 the Spanish government declared it a national monument; and in 1984 it was included by UNESCO in the list of works belonging to the Heritage of Mankind.

It was at the turn of the century that Eusebi Güell entrusted Gaudí with this ambitious, innovative project. Work would continue until 1914, the year in which they came to a definitive halt. The maecenas travelled frequently to England, and although we have no documentary evidence in favour of the hypothesis, it is believed that there he conceived the idea of creating not only a garden city but also a private residential district. While it is true that sixty-two spacious and previously delimited private properties were anticipated for the Park Güell, together with a number of community services such as a caretaker, lighting, streets, a market, a public square and even the height of each property wall, it is equally true that no thought was ever given to any other kind of services such as schools, theatres, hospitals, sports fields or churches. When Güell entrusted Gaudí with the project, he had already acquired two large rural estates in the Gràcia district, in the area popularly known as the Muntanya Pelada, which together occupied a site of fifteen hectares. These estates were between 450 and 630 feet above sea level, that is, at a relatively considerable height which afforded attractive views over Barcelona.

As from 1901 and during a space of two years, the principal and only task consisted of levelling the land. In a display of characteristic good sense, Gaudí

The anagram was significantly written in English.

By virtue of its shape and decoration, the bench is the Park's main attraction.

*While the bench maintains a constant rhythm,
the ornamentation is a permanent source of surprises.*

*Gaudí provided the lizard with
the original form he desired.*

did not want to intervene too much in the landscape: he therefore ordered only the most indispensable earthworks and excavations. This criterion obliged him to trace out a gentle network of streets which, wherever possible, followed the contours of the land. The only exceptions to this were the viaducts, but since they were built from local stone and endowed with forms inspired by nature, they merged perfectly well, as if camouflaged, with their surroundings.

Apart from the show house, the first home to be built was for Martí Trias, based on a project by the architect Juli Batllevell and completed in 1906. That same year the architect Francesc Berenguer designed the house for Gaudí's father and family; although Francesc Gaudí died shortly afterwards, his son remained in the house until 1925, when he decided never to move from the site of the Sagrada Família. In 1910 Eusebi Güell entrusted Gaudí with the refurbishment of the historical Casa Larrard in Can Muntaner, where the maecenas died in 1918. These were the only plots ever sold. Such resounding failure could not possibly have been equalled.

In 1922 Güell's heirs offered the site to the City Hall, who purchased it, converted it into a municipal park and opened it to the public the following year. Gaudí's house was acquired in 1961 by the private society Amics de Gaudí, where they now have their headquarters and a small sample of the architect's works and memorabilia.

Access to the park is by the main gate, in Carrer d'Olot. A great rubblework wall with an undulating top and covered with ceramic fragments borders the edge of the park in this sector. Two large ceramic medallions display the name of the place and reveal certain English connotations in the form of the use of the word "Park". On either side, one Gaudinian construction each, one conceived as the services pavilion and the other as the caretaker's lodge. The lodge has recently been refurbished as a book and souvenir shop, its false ceiling having been lowered and the partitions removed to reveal a highly creative interior. Both houses have a similar air, both being crowned by cowls which immediately bring to mind the hallucinatory mushroom *amanita muscaria* and remind us of children's stories in the style of the Brothers Grimm.

Immediately behind we come to the foot of a solemn staircase that takes us on a gentle uphill initiatory climb, the main landmark of which being a medallion with a serpent's head emerging from the Catalan coat of arms. Next we come across one of the emblematic pieces: the giant lizard that guards the place. We are assured that Gaudí, once he had completed the iron skeleton which

The crowning elements of the porter's lodge are more sculptural than architectural.

would support the body of the beast and its *trencadís* decoration, jumped up and down on it several times to break its domed shape and give it the capriciously warped form which endows the torso with expressive power. Immediately behind we have the hollow at the foot of the temple, the fantastic animal's cave which visitors may use to take a rest along their way.

We now enter the Doric temple or hypostyle hall, originally designed to be the market place. A magic place featuring the avant-garde master work of the architect Josep Maria Jujol, who covered most of the ceiling with fascinating rosaries. He used not only the trencadís technique but also that of collage, applying the ends of broken bottles, cups, glasses and a doll's head. All this he created in 1909, that is, some years before the Cubists.

Above we may admire Gaudí and Jujol's masterpiece: the serpentine bench that borders the large esplanade. It was Gaudí who created the form of the bench, based on prefabricated modules, by means of the exemplary technique of determining the dimensions of the modules on the measurements of one of the workers. The bench was built between 1910 and 1913, that is, before Kandinsky painted his first abstract watercolour. The bench is therefore the first abstract piece in the history of art, although further merits are its dimensions, its public character and its high cost. Completely uninhibited, and giving free rein to his imagination and automatic impulses, Jujol made a composition on the basis of polychrome *trencadís* that decomposes colours and forms. Here and there collage also appears, based on crockery from his father's house and other elements. He even included graffiti (which were not discovered until 1961!), consisting of the insertion of Marian prayers and of cross-like motifs.

From the Greek Theatre plaza a number of paths lead off, made of local stone and responding to a will to evoke the forms of nature, ranging from palm trees to flower pots. Thus the viaduct bearing walls are endowed with forms, inclinations and arches which are true discoveries. Those intrigued by the fact that the Carretera del Carmel is lined by large stone spheres should stone and count them: they will discover that their number corresponds to that of the beads of a rosary: one hundred and fifty.

Jujol's imaginative polychrome endows this ceiling with unwonted power.

The fascinating space created by the parabolic arches.

41

BELLESGUARD, LA CASA FIGUERAS

Bellesguard was chosen and thus christened by the last in the line of the Catalan Crown, Martí I. Such a wise choice was undoubtedly influenced by Bernat Metge, a writer and influential figure at court. There are reasons that explain why the king, who was so esteemed by his subjects that he was rechristened Martí ''l'humà'' (Martí the Humane), became so enamoured of this spot. His health was shattered, his lungs in particular being in such a poor state that he had difficulty in breathing; but his condition improved as soon as he found himself in a well ventilated and above all dry climate. Thus, when the king was taken to this spot and was able to admire its fine view over his beloved Barcelona, he did not hesitate in calling it Bellesguard, which confirms the beauty of what could be contemplated from there. Enthusiastic and resolute, in 1408 he ordered a summer residence to be built, although given its proximity to the city he would frequently visit it even when not oppressed by the summer heat. Bellesguard became a major historical residence, by virtue not only of the long time the king resided there but also of the fact that it was visited by a considerable number of crowned heads and leading dignitaries; suffice it to say that among these was Pope Benedict XIII. The extinction of that royal house and other historical misfortunes led to the abandonment of such a noble residence and its subsequent deterioration and collapse.

When Maria Sagués, the widow of Jaume Figueras, entrusted Gaudí with the Bellesguard project, all that was left of the former royal residence was the remains of two towers and a crenellated wall. This was more than enough for the architect, however, since he would thus

be able to work in total freedom, while these remaining fragments would give wings to his imagination. Evidence of this is the fact that the work he created is a free though respectful evocation of and homage to that past greatness which, however Gothic and regal it may have been, could not leave a man of his talents indifferent.

He began the project in 1900, although for reasons which we need not go into here work was not finished until 1916. The first thing he did was reconstruct the historical wall and build a viaduct which would allow him to divert the path that crossed the estate. This single-family dwelling was conceived as a fifteen-metre sided square with windows on all four façades and an emerging prismatic body with a tower-belvedere crowned by a needle. The exterior attracts the observer's attention by virtue of the way in which it blends with the landscape and the construction is made entirely out of rubblework, with small fragments of locally extracted slate. The openings are relatively few in walls which evoke the past, although all of them, together with the semicircular arches, the narrow tapering and twin windows should be interpreted as the architect's own personal homage to the Catalan Gothic. If the top floor is the most striking, it is surpassed in spectacularity by a tower and a needle which ''hoists'' his particular version of the Catalan flag, which here acquires a significance to be borne in mind. While in Casa Vicens Gaudí evoked the Mudejar, not only surpassing it but creating a piece in his own inimitable style, in Bellesguard he paid homage to a regal Gothic without ceasing to be Gaudí. It is a real shame that the interior cannot be visited, since in terms of composition

*Both the interior spaces
and the exterior forms are
a lesson in functional art.*

and itinerary it anticipates by several decades what Le Corbusier claimed to have invented, namely the *promenade architectonique*. While this house is truly innovative from the aesthetic point of view, it also reflects the imperious need on the part of the architect to reflect on structural problems while making no attempt to conceal them; on the contrary, Gaudí made full use of their aesthetic potential. White walls, light filtered through stained-glass windows, unexpected spaces in a naked rubblework loft and freestanding arcades are some of the elements which contribute to the creation of a highly suggestive atmosphere.

Collaborating with Gaudí on this project was the architect Domènec Sugrañes i Gras who, with the consent of the master, carried out a number of rather unfortunate interventions; perhaps the most aggressive of these are the mosaics on the backrests to the benches against the wall, thoroughly out of place in such a context of modernity. The fact that the house is in such a fine state of repair today is thanks to its present owners, the family of Lluís Aguilera, whose unflagging efforts in this direction have occasionally led to their having to bear onerous financial burdens.

THE RESTORATION
OF MALLORCA CATHEDRAL

The new baldachin suspended over the main altar.

Bishop Campins, who was responsible for the diocese of Palma, wished totally to restore the Cathedral, although he was not sure how it should be done or by whom. One day he visited the Sagrada Família, where he conversed with Gaudí. So astonished was he by the architect's knowledge of and interest in liturgy that he commissioned him to carry out the task.

Gaudí presented a very complete project, later complemented by a highly detailed model. The project consisted basically of dismantling the large altarpieces, moving the choir to the presbytery, opening the Trinity Chapel, creating a new pulpit and a new choir, opening boarded-up Gothic windows, stretching a baldachin over the main altar, restoring the stained-glass rose window, completing the decoration with paintings in the choir pews, furniture (folding stairs, bench, stools and liturgical objects) and wrought iron.

The first part of the project had been completed by 1904. The second was never completed, however, due to the avant-garde style used by Gaudí and Jujol and, above all, to the death of Bishop Campins, who had financed the work.

The intervention of the two architects was highly audacious, and it need not surprise us that most of the ecclesiastics of the time were thoroughly scandalised by it. However, the passing of time has confirmed the extraordinary quality of the work they carried out.

While Gaudí's genius was viewed with mistrust, the freedom with which Jujol worked and the results of his intervention caused true indignation. Indeed, on the backs of the choir pews it was not long before openly abstract compositions appeared. The young priest Emili Sagristà, the bishop's assistant, witnessed how the results were obtained and described the process in a text: Gaudí would sit watching Jujol at the height of his feverish, automatic activity, pioneer of future Tachisme, from time to time asking the master for his opinion. Gaudí

Details of the presbytery railings, the archbishop's coat-of-arms and the new wrought-iron chandelier.

would urge him on: ''That's fine, Jujol, just fine!'' It is said that the ecclesiastics would gather in the harbour waiting for the arrival of Rubió, a Barcelona architect assigned to the Cathedral, to implore him to liberate them once and for all from Gaudí and Jujol.

CASA BATLLÓ

Elegant Passeig de Gràcia enhances the extraordinary quality of this work.

In 1904, José Batlló asked Gaudí to design a house on elegant Passeig de Gràcia. The architect, instead of demolishing the existing one, created the two façades, the porter's lodge, the inner patio, the semi-basement and the ground and first floors. The remained of the structure and the second, third, fourth and fifth floors were left as they were.

Gaudí devoted himself enthusiastically to the project and gave free rein to his imagination and ingenuity. The citizens closely followed the progress of the work, for to an extent they had acquired the habit of disparaging Gaudí's genius. They were astonished by the result: as soon as they could observe that façade they christened it *La Casa dels Ossos* (The House of Bones). And they were not far wrong; furthermore, they were better oriented than a number of commentators who have interpreted it as an evocation either of Carnival or the sea. The former thought they saw Carnival in the masks (balustrades), the confetti (the multi-coloured façade) and Harlequin's hat (the top). The latter interpreted the astonishing coloured cladding of the façade as a liberal view of the sea which bathes the shallow coves of the Costa Brava. To the first I would reply that a mystic such as Gaudí would never have employed such a pagan and anticlerical recourse as Carnival, especially since he placed a cross in a prominent position at the top of the façade. Going back to what I said before, the *Casa dels Ossos* is far more appropriate, particularly if one bears in mind that the ironwork was originally painted an ivory colour and the recently quarried stone from which the bottom part of the house is built was of a natural vanilla tone. The people were on the mark, therefore, since the symbology which I detect in such a spectacular ensemble is an evocation of the legend of St. George, Patron Saint of Catalonia. His presence would seem to be embodied in the huge tower, placed off-centre in order to converse

better with its neighbour, Casa Amatller. The tower can be seen as the image of the lance, crowned by the cross, symbolising the religious principle so beloved to Gaudí of Good triumphing over Evil. It need not surprise us, therefore, that the main body of the tower features the huge gilt initials alluding to Jesus (JHS) and Mary (M). The lance has mortally wounded the dragon, represented here by the crest and the scales which cover its skin and fill almost the whole of the façade. The wound is the hollow which can be perceived near the spinal column, the edges of which are coloured blood red. In the meantime, the balcony

Colours in the patio are graduated in direct relation to the natural light it receives from above.

balustrades are reminiscent of the eye sockets of skulls, while the forms Gaudí employed to create most of the lower part of the façade bring to mind the bones of the victims devoured by the dragon. This might therefore be a reasonable explanation why these are perhaps the only balustrades in the whole of Barcelona which are not inevitably painted black.

From the entrance hall a staircase leads directly up to the first floor where the owner, Batlló, lived. His residence was meticulously conceived by Gaudí, who thus obtained his most unitary habitat if we ignore the Palau Güell. Despite the fact that until recently this was the head office of an insurance company, the building's owners, the inimitable atmosphere still persists. We must nevertheless turn our mind's eye back to earlier times to imagine the ambience with its fireside, almost three-dimensional doors, the altar, the chairs, ceilings with bas-reliefs, the metalwork and so on. In short, everything contributed to transmitting the idea of a total work. One of Batlló's grandchildren by marriage once told me that Gaudí had asked him how many men and how many women were in the family; as the question surprised the client's wife somewhat, Gaudí explained that he intended to design a different chair for each sex, which was a far from outrageous idea since it was attire he was thinking of rather than anatomy. Mrs Batlló would have none of it, however, and thus Gaudí designed the ''unisex'' chairs which can be admired today. Outstanding craftsmen contributed the best of their respective talents to the project: the Badía brothers were responsible for the wrought iron; the firm of Casas y Bardés for the joinery; Hijo de P. Pujol Baucís for the tiling; Sebastià Ribó for the ceramics; Josep Pelegrí for the stained glass. The discs for the façade and the cladding for the cross were from Manacor. The carpentry for the main-façade windows

The carpentry establishes an unusual dialogue between the noble wood and the glass.

The fireplace provides an unexpected inner space of curious intimacy.

The suggestive interplay between chimneys constitutes the highly creative crowning element of the rear façade.

is not only outstanding but also innovative.

As regards the intervention of Jujol, which is not documented, I believe I detect it above all in the abstract ornamentation of the main façade, in this case as gestural as it is *tachiste* and thoroughly characteristic of an imagination governed by liberty, never by restraint; by improvisation, never by calculation; by provocative and openly avant-garde spontaneity. Joan Bassegoda and Antonio González deny that Jujol ever intervened; on the other hand, the curators of the exhibition devoted to him organised by the Collegi d'Arquitectes, Ignasi de Solà-Morales and Flores contend that he did contribute to the polychrome decoration of the façade. My opinion is based on the stylistic coherence I seem to detect in his interventions.

This house also invites us to discover and enjoy a *promenade architectonique* from long before Le Corbusier invented it, beginning in the vestibule, it continues up the private staircase, enters the landing, continues through the waiting room and ends in the private rooms.

Certain elements, despite their simplicity and essentialness, are nonetheless worthy of admiration, such as the colour graduation in the interior patio, which ranges from deep blue to white depending on the intensity of the natural light. The rear façade, although it is not so spectacular, reveals the architect's interest in leaving traces of his personality. By virtue both of the combination of openings and solids and of the multicoloured ornamentation, it deserves contemplation. The treatment given to the unusual spaces at the top, the fruit of such an unexpected form, deserves a chapter to itself. The recently restored loft exudes a rare atmosphere in which the potency of the structures is revealed. The solution given to the groups of chimneys is highly creative and would teach its culmination point in Casa Milà.

The current owner lets the ground and first floors for meetings, conventions and all manner of social and tourist functions, thanks to which the people of Barcelona and lovers of Gaudí's work have the opportunity to visit a private property which was hitherto closed to them.

The powerful, provocative image of the spectacular crowning of the main façade.

CASA MILÀ, LA PEDRERA

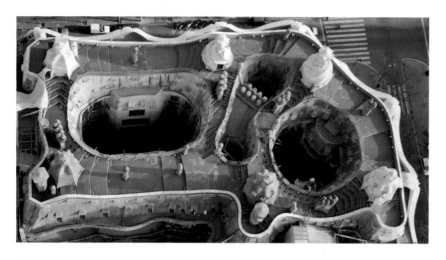

*Bird's-eye-view of the roof
and view of the main façade.*

*The wrought-iron railings
were the avant-garde, gestural
and improvised creation of
Jujol, who thus showed that
it was possible to make
sculpture out of iron, a
lesson that Gargallo and
Gonzàlez soon learnt.*

There are those who have seen in Casa Milà an evocation of sea waves and those who contend that it is a mountain, crowned by a cloud as a kind of gigantic pedestal to enthrone the image of the Virgin. I believe, however, that from to-day's viewpoint this imposing edifice impresses us for what it is: a total abstract work. I also believe, however, that he was inspired by the original mountain of Sant Sadurní which rises above Gallifa (where Miró and Llorens Artigas created so many ceramic pieces), impressed by the discovery he made while residing for a few months in Sant Feliu de Codines to escape from the cholera epidemic that raged in Barcelona in 1885.

It is important to note that his collaborator Jujol was the author of the balcony parapets: each one is a different piece, improvised in the forge, and there is a considerable difference between the gestural design of these parapets and the modular quality of the two main doors on the ground floor, characteristic of Gaudí. As soon as Jujol's work was finished, two Catalan sculptors, Pau Gargallo and Juli Gonzàlez, discovered that it was possible to use iron, and it is for this reason that they were the first to give this material, never before employed in sculpture, its rightful lace in the history of art. Moreover, it was Gonzàlez who taught Picasso this technique.

La Pedrera is in fact two buildings, arranged around two curvilinear central patios, each with its own independent entrance door. The façade is composed of large blocks of stone from Garraf and Vilafranca. Each of the blocks was dressed on site and then fitted into the ensemble, which often meant that major corrections had to be made. The same asymmetry that governs the façade also characterises the interior, precisely in the form of the wavy line that separates the two bodies: the six habitable floors and the two-storey loft, where Gaudí placed the invocation to Mary ("Ave gratia M plena Dominus tecum") and

*Gaudí's modular style is particularly
evident in the main entrance.*

the rose bud that alludes to the Virgin. Above the initial and to crown the building, Gaudí had intended to place an enormous image of the Virgin and Child, modelled by the sculptor Mani. The owner did not like it, however, so the idea never left the project stage, which is a good thing for the realistic style and poor artistic quality of the piece were thoroughly out of context with the rest.

On the roof we see that Gaudí had learnt much from his experiences with the Palau Güell, although with a substantial and more fruitful version of its earlier counterpart, in which the architect adopted an openly and more committed avant-garde stance through the creation of more striking forms and volumes with an imposing presence that impresses even those who observe the top of the building from the street. The roof consists of several different levels, although in fact they can be grouped together in terms of three functions: stair entrances, ventilation shafts and chimneys. The stair entrances are the largest, adopting the form of huts crowned by helmets. The cladding used to face these warped surfaces is the usual one of broken marble fragments. The ventilators adopt a form which heralds the abstract sculpture of coming decades, while the multiplication of openings confers greater importance on empty rather than filled areas. The chimneys are more forceful when grouped together. The original cladding of one of them consists of fragments of champagne bottles.

The building was acquired by the Caixa de Catalunya savings bank, who decided to carry out meticulous restoration work. Most laudable here is the recovery of the attics, which must be visited in order to admire the whole roof structure, which although in brick is unforgettable. Chillida declared that this space is music.

Also worth a visit is the first floor, which the Caixa de Catalunya has refurbished as an exhibition hall. The columns, all different, and the ceiling are exquisite examples of Jujol's work, originally conceived for the residence of the owner, Pedro Milà. His wife, Rosario Segimon, had never liked Gaudí's work, and when the architect died suddenly in 1926, she had the whole decor changed to the typically nouveau-riche Louis XV style.

The colour and originality of the crowning elements endow the patios with great personality.

For the roof Gaudí created a number of forms that must be interpreted as heralding the best abstract sculpture that was yet to come.

THE TEMPLE OF THE SAGRADA FAMILIA

The towers are an eye-catching identity sign.

*Gaudí managed to complete
the Birth façade.*

The Sagrada Família temple is Gaudí's most famous, though not his best, work, so ambitious that from the very outset it seemed probable that it would never be finished. It occupies a whole block in Barcelona's Eixample, bounded by Carrer de Mallorca, Carrer de Provença and Carrer de Sardenya.

The origin of the temple is the initiative of bookseller Josep Maria Bocabella, a pious worshipper of St. Joseph. The Mercedarian friar Josep Maria Rodríguez proposed the construction of a temple in 1874. To this end, he hired the architect Francisco de Paula del Villar, who drew up a Neogothic project. Work began in 1882 with a subterranean crypt, but technical discrepancies soon arose, culminating in Paula del Villar's resignation and Gaudí's taking over the project, to which he devoted the rest of his life. Indeed, during his last two years he actually lived on site.

Gaudí completely modified the project in terms not only of aesthetics but also of dimensions. His immediate ambition was to erect the Birth façade.

The Sagrada Família is a temple of Gothic-basilican ground plan in the form of a Latin cross, with five lengthwise naves, and an apsis nave, all enveloped by an exterior cloister. Beyond the grandiosity of the project, Gaudí's ambitions here were vertical: an Apotheosis given visual form in no less than eighteen spires (twelve to evoke the Apostles, four for the Evangelists and two for the Virgin and Christ), the tallest of which soars above the dome and is crowned at a height of 510 feet by a three-dimensional cross. The remaining two façades are consecrated to Death and Resurrection.

The east façade is arranged around three main doors, in the following order: Hope, Charity and Faith. This is all that Gaudí was able to finish himself. His idea was to compose a true Nativity scene with a profusion of realist and highly didactic sculptures on the mystery,

The tall towers act as original frames of the urban landscape.

The polychrome cypress is a suggestive piece of sculpture.

The potent spiral staircase that climbs up the tower.

The sculpture is the product of several different techniques. The result is also diverse from the point of view of artistic quality.

although their artistic quality is rather poor. The green colour of the enormous cypress, thanks to which the tree stands out against the rest of the ensemble, attests to Gaudí's intention to use all the façade's Montjuïc sandstone merely as a support for total polychrome, which can be observed also on the crowning elements of the towers.

When he died suddenly in 1926, Gaudí had left no complete, detailed plans of the temple as a whole and, as if this were not enough, at the outbreak of the Civil War what documentation there was, together with models, plans and other material, was burnt. As from 1949, however, thanks on the one hand to donations and on the other to revenue from the entrance fees charged to temple visitors, work was resumed and proceeded at an ever faster pace. In the mid sixties a manifesto was published, signed by numerous personalities from both the Spanish and international cultural milieus, headed by Le Corbusier, asking for construction work to be halted. The controversy was rekindled in 1986 when the sculptor Subirachs was commissioned to sculpt the large ensemble to preside over the Passion façade. The highly personal nature of the sculptor's work has given rise to heated arguments for and against. Within the precinct of the Sagrada Família, beside Carrer Mallorca, stand the Parish Schools, an example of Gaudí's mastery when it came to providing solutions to the lack of funds. On a ground plan of ten by twenty metres, he erected two partitions to create three classrooms. The building is presided over by curves, which allowed the architect to do away with bearing walls. Le Corbusier was so astonished when he discovered this work in 1928 that he did not hesitate to make a number of sketches of such an unprecedented construction.

This profile has become a worldwide symbol of Barcelona.

INDEX OF WORKS

ESSENTIAL BIBLIOGRAPHY

BASSEGODA NONELL, Juan. *Gaudí*. Salvat, Barcelona, 1985.
—*La Pedrera de Gaudí*. Caixa de Catalunya, Barcelona. 1987.
—*El gran Gaudí*. Ausa, Sabadell, 1989.

BERGÓS, Joan. *Antoni Gaudí: l'home i l'obra*. Ariel, Barcelona, 1954.

BOHIGAS, Oriol. *Arquitectura modernista*. Lumen, Barcelona, 1968.

CASANELLAS, Enric. *Nueva visión de Gaudí*. Polígrafa, Barcelona, 1964.

CIRICI PELLICER, Alexandre. *El arte modernista catalán*. Aymà, Barcelona, 1951.

CIRLOT, Juan Eduardo. *El arte de Gaudí*. Omega, Barcelona, 1950.

Several authors. *Josep Maria Jujol, arquitecte. 1879-1949*. Col·legi d'Arquitectes, Barcelona, 1989.
—*El Palau Güell*. Diputació de Barcelona, Barcelona, 1990.

FLORES, Carlos. *Gaudí, Jujol y el modernismo catalán*. Aguilar, Madrid, 1982.

MARTINELL, César: *Gaudinismo*. Amigos de Gaudí, Barcelona, 1954.
—*Gaudí: su vida, su teoría, su obra*. Colegio de Arquitectos, Barcelona, 1967.

PERMANYER, Lluís. *Història de l'Eixample*. Plaza y Janés, Barcelona, 1991.
—*Cites i testimonis sobre Barcelona*. La Campana, Barcelona, 1993.
—*Biografia del Passeig de Gràcia*. 1994.
—*Gaudí of Barcelona*. Polígrafa, Barcelona, 1997

PUJOLS, Francesc; Salvador DALÍ; Robert DESCHARNES; Clovis PREVOST. *La visió artística i religiosa de Gaudí*. Aymà, Barcelona, 1969.

RÀFOLS, Josep Francesc. *Modernismo y modernistas*. Destino, Barcelona, 1949.

SOLÀ-MORALES, Ignasi de. *Gaudí*. Polígrafa, Barcelona, 1983.